"R" Daily Devotional
40 Days of Restoration

Jamal E. Quinn

A publication of ML Excellence

Copyright 2019
ISBN: 978-1-7336219-2-2
Jamal E. Quinn

All rights reserved.
No portion of this book may be used
without the written permission of the publisher.
It is protected under copyright laws.
Scripture quotations marked NKJV are taken
from the New King James Version.
Copyright 1982 by Thomas Nelson.
Used by permission. All rights reserved.
Scripture quotations marked KJV are taken
from the King James Version.

Table of Contents

Introduction..5
Day 1 – Repentance...8
Day 2 – Revival..9
Day 3 – Return...10
Day 4 – Restoration...11
Day 5 – Renew...12
Day 6 – Refresh...13
Day 7 – Rest...14
Day 8 – Recover..15
Day 9 – Remember..16
Day 10 – Release...17
Day 11 – Resurrection...18
Day 12 – Revive...19
Day 13 – Reconcile..20
Day 14 – Render..21
Day 15 – Revelation..22
Day 16 – Reward...23
Day 17 – Reap..24
Day 18 – Righteousness..25
Day 19 – Riches...26
Day 20 – Recall..27
Day 21 – Rain...28
Day 22 – Run..29

Day 23 – Resist...30
Day 24 – Resist - Part 2....................................31
Day 25 – Reprove 32
Day 26 – Rebuke...33
Day 27 – Rebuke - Part 2..................................34
Day 28 – Reaching..35
Day 29 – Respect..36
Day 30 – Rock...37
Day 31 – Refuge..38
Day 32 – Rise..39
Day 33 – Reverse..40
Day 34 – Relieve...41
Day 35 – Replenish...42
Day 36 – Rejoice...43
Day 37 – Refine...44
Day 38 – Regeneration.....................................45
Day 39 –Rescue..46
Day 40 – Recompense......................................47
About the Author..49

Introduction

Greetings and God Bless! First of all I want to give honor, glory and praise to the Lord Jesus Christ for the opportunity to write *"R" Daily Devotional, 40 Days of Restoration*. This devotional is for anyone that has a desire to draw nearer to the Lord, with a hunger and thirst after righteousness. The scriptures declare in James 4:8 – "Draw near to God and he will draw near to you." Jesus said in Matt 5:6 – "Blessed are those who hunger and thirst for righteousness, for they shall be filled."

It is so important that every believer understand that we do not live by bread alone but by every Word of God. (Matt 4:4 and Luke 4:4) Each day of this devotional is presented with an encouraging and inspiring Word from the scriptures that begin with the letter "R," which will provide encouragement, restoration and blessing to fill your day.

There are two reasons for writing this devotional. The first reason is because I understand the times that we live in, we are busier than ever. We live in a microwave society where we don't have much time for anything, but one thing we must make time for is the Word of God! It is so essential for your spiritual growth and edification in Christ!

When the Lord Jesus was in the desert, he fasted for 40 days praying unto the Father, and endured the temptations of the devil. He overcame Satan by standing on the Word of God and saying, "It is written!" After his 40 days of temptations and testing, the bible says in Luke 4:14, "Then Jesus returned in the power of the Spirit to Galilee, and news of Him went out through all the surrounding region." Some of your greatest victories will come after you have been challenged by what I call the five pains of life. They are trials, tribulations, temptations, tests, and troubles, but you will overcome them by your perseverance and standing on the Word of God.

The second reason for writing this book is after you have overcome trials, tribulations, temptations, tests and troubles, the Lord restores you. There is a theme throughout the bible that anyone that the LORD has called for a specific purpose went through one of the five pains of life. After you go through and get the victory, there is always restoration. King David after being anointed King had to run for his life from Saul and lived in the desert, but after a period of time. He was restored. Job went through a devastating time with his health, his family, his finances and his friends, but God restored him. Joseph went from the pit, to a prison and eventually landed in a palace after God restored him.

I have personally experienced and witnessed restoration from the Lord during trials, tribulations, temptations, tests and troubles as well. So I speak from experience and not only from what I have read! As a young child at the age of five, I was very sick due to meningitis. It was a very serious illness that could have resulted in death, but through much prayer, God healed and restored me. In 1973, my mother who nursed and cared for me during my illness passed away at age twenty eight. As a child at the age of seven years old, I was devastated.
I carried the memory of my mother's death for many years and it was very painful, but God restored me.

In January 2014, my wife had a serious medical situation. Through all of this I was in full time ministry with a growing church and congregation that eventually dwindled down to a few faithful members, but I continued to do ministry through it all. Then in 2016, many of our key leaders left the church unexpectedly. These were very challenging times of my life, but the Lord restored me through it all!

Today, I can testify today that my wife is healed, and the church is doing well! I can honestly say we have experienced the wonderful restoration of God!

I now understand what David meant in Psalm 23:1-3 when he said, "The Lord is my shepherd, I shall not want; he makes me to lie down in green pastures. He leads me beside the still waters. He **restores** my soul. He leads me in the paths of righteousness for his name's sake.

This devotional can be used during a time of fasting and consecration, a daily devotional to uplift you in 40 days, or just a word of encouragement to bless your day! Get ready to be blessed and empowered by "R" Daily Devotional: 40 Days of Restoration!

Day 1 – Repentance

If my people who are called by my name will humble themselves, and pray and seek my face, and turn from their wicked ways, then I will hear from heaven, and will forgive their sin and heal their land.
2 Chronicles 7: 14

One of the prerequisites for restoration and blessing from the Lord is Godly sorrow and heartfelt repentance. This scripture is often quoted but the significance of it is powerful if we apply it to our lives. Solomon had just completed the building of the Lord's house which was the temple and he prayed to the Lord. The Lord then said, "I have heard your prayer," but here is the prerequisite for my blessing when I shut up heaven; "If My people who are called by My name will humble themselves, and pray and seek My face, and turn from their wicked ways, then I will hear from heaven, and will forgive their sin and heal their land. (2 Chron 7:14) Now my eyes will be open and my ears attentive to prayer made in this place. (2 Chron 7:15)   There are four things we must always remember as a prerequisite to see the hand of God move: humility, prayer, seeking the face of God, and turning from sin. When we do these things, the LORD said, "I will hear from heaven, forgive your sin and heal your land." Repentance is the key to revival, restoration and healing. Today take time to examine yourself, confess and repent of anything that would cause you to fall short of the glory of God.

Day 2 – Revival

I am afflicted very much; revive me, O LORD, according to your word.
Psalm 119:107

The Word revival comes from the word revive which means to restore life, consciousness, resuscitate, regain life or strength. We find the word revive in many verses of scripture especially in the Psalms. The writer of the Psalms was humble enough to recognize that at times we need to be revived or as we say today; a revival. We need a fresh touch of God's presence and power when we have lost our way. When something requires resuscitation it must be revived.

Today it is no secret that many churches need a revival. When we look at the book of Revelation in chapters 2-3, the Lord sent seven letters to seven churches. Only two of those churches received commendation; Philadelphia and Smyrna. Five of those churches had lost their way. They needed a revival in Jesus name! Our heavenly Father has given us his Son Jesus Christ who has given us salvation through his blood. He is the only one that can revive us. When we turn to the Lord in humility and repentance, and stand strong in the Word, he will restore us, and cause his face to shine upon us. Today cry out to the Lord for a revival in the church, and in our personal lives, that we may experience the presence and power of God like never before!

Day 3 – Return

For you were like sheep going astray, but have now returned to the Shepherd and Overseer of your souls.
1 Peter 2:25

Restoration begins when something is returned to its original condition or to a better state than it was before. The bible says in Isaiah 53:6, "All we like sheep have gone astray; we have turned everyone to his own way." During the creation week of Genesis, the bible says in Gen 1:31, "And God saw everything that he had made, and, behold, it was very good." The world and many believers are in the condition they are in today because they have turned to our own way. If we return to the Lord, he will return to us. Zec 1:3 says, "Therefore say to them, "Thus says the LORD of hosts, return to me, says the LORD of hosts, and I will return to you," Says the LORD of hosts." When we return to the Lord who is the Shepherd and Overseer of our souls, he will return to us and we will experience a refreshing peace and revival in our lives like never before. Today, let us return to the LORD with all your heart! For he is the Good Shepherd (John 10:11), Great Shepherd (Heb 13:20), and Chief Shepherd! (1 Peter 5:4). The LORD has promised in his Word that if we return to him, he will return to us!

Day 4 - Restoration

He restores my soul; he leads me in paths of righteousness for his name's sake.
Psalm 23:3

One of the most beloved Psalms is Psalms 23 in which David proclaims, "The Lord is my Shepherd, I shall not want. He makes me to lie down in green pastures. He leads me beside the still waters. " (Psalm 23:1-2) I want you to visualize the picture of a peaceful serene green field. Can you see it? He leads me beside the still waters. Can you see it? Still and calm waters have such a refreshing and calming effect on us. They are not rushing or flowing waters, but cool, calm and collective waters that are still. David then says, "He restores my soul."(Psalm 23:3) Restore means to bring back into existence, or reestablish, or to bring back to an original or normal condition. No matter where you may be today, or what you are going through. The Lord desires to restore you spiritually, physically, mentally, emotionally, financially and personally. Today open your mouth and proclaim as David did, "The Lord is your Shepherd!" Say out of your mouth with confidence, "He restores my soul." Today is the beginning of restoration in your life. The Lord desires to restore you in the midst of every trial or tribulation that would steal your joy, peace and strength. Today let the Good Shepherd restore your soul because he is a wonderful Shepherd who will keep you eternally safe from hurt, harm and danger!

Day 5 – Renew

Create in me a clean heart, O God; and renew a right spirit within me.
Psalm 51:10

Many of us know the story of King David, a man who the Bible says was after God's heart. (Acts 13:22) David was a good man, but just like any man he was prone to temptation and to sin. Many times people ask how a man who committed sin be a man after God's heart. When we look at the character and life of David, he was humble and had a good heart. (1 Sam 16:7) David loved the LORD but had a moment in the flesh, which caused him a lot of trouble. The thing about David was that he was truly repentant for his actions. When we read Psalm 51, it speaks of the character and life of a man who was broken, repentant, and sorrowful for his actions. David cried out to the Lord and said, "Create in me a clean heart 'O' God and renew a right spirit within me." David knew that the spirit that caused him to sin was not the Spirit of God, but an act in the flesh. Jer 17:9 says, "The heart is deceitful above all things, and desperately wicked; who can know it?" The Lord restored David and he is known as one of the greatest Kings that ever reigned in Israel. You may not be in sin today, but there will be a time when you need to be renewed with the refreshing presence of the Holy Spirit. Today, ask the LORD to renew you with his spirit!

Day 6 – Refresh

Therefore repent and convert so that your sins may be blotted out, when the times of refreshing shall come from the presence of the Lord.
Act 3:19

Isn't it wonderful when you can enjoy a fresh shower after a long day at work, or maybe working in the yard? It could be a fresh warm or cool shower depending on how you feel! After the shower you feel refreshed from the toil of the day. The Apostle Peter in a sense is conveying the same idea except the dirt comes from sin. He admonishes the people to repent and be converted, and to turn to the Lord that that sin would be blotted out or removed. After humility, repentance and turning to the Lord, we will experience a refreshing presence from the Lord where the stain of sin has been blotted out and forgiven. In other words when we repent and turn from sin, we are forgiven and we experience his wonderful presence. Psalm 16:11 says, "In Your presence is fullness of joy; at your right hand are pleasures forevermore." We experience the wonderful presence of the LORD when we are refreshed. Today rejoice in the Lord and be refreshed with his wonderful presence.

Day 7 – Rest

And on the seventh day God ended His work which He had made. And He rested on the seventh day from all His work which He had made. And God blessed the seventh day and sanctified it, because in it He had rested from all His work which God created to make.
Genesis 2: 2-3

It's interesting to note in the Bible that God in all his perfect ways created everything good from the first to the sixth day. On the seventh day He rested. It's amazing that even our sovereign God, Yehovah even understood the importance of rest. Why is it that many times in our social media, get it done, quick fast and in a hurry society, we do not understand this? Each and every one of us needs rest. Your body is not a machine. It is the temple of the Holy Spirit in whom Christ dwells. (1 Corinthian 6: 19) We must take care of this body which needs rest to be restored to full strength. I must admit I am guilty of this, but I have learned to rest in the midst of multiple responsibilities. The Bible says that God rested on the seventh day. I believe this is the standard for which God has set for us. It doesn't matter whether we believe the Sabbath day is Saturday or Sunday. The most important thing is that you take the time to stop, rest, get a good night's sleep, read a book, go to the park, get some exercise and be restored. You may be in ministry, or working a forty hour week, but today the Word of the LORD is rest in Jesus Name!

Day 8 – Recover

> Is there no balm in Gilead; is there no physician there? Why then is not the health of the daughter of my people recovered?
> Jeremiah 8:22

Jeremiah the Prophet asked a valid question because the people of God were in a backslidden condition experiencing pain and hurt. They did not heed the voice of the Lord, and every man was turned to his own way. The question is valid even today. If you were to injure yourself, wisdom says to seek relief and healing because of the pain. Jeremiah knew there was an abundance of balm in Gilead, a healing salve or ointment and physicians to apply it. Yet the people received it not. Jesus the Great Physician has provided the healing ointment and balm required for all sickness and sin. He did it at the cross by shedding his blood and providing a way of salvation. Jesus said in Luke 4:18, "The Spirit of the Lord is upon me, because he has anointed me to preach the gospel to the poor; he has sent me to heal the brokenhearted, to preach deliverance to the captives, and recovering of sight to the blind, to set at liberty them that are bruised." Jesus paid the price with his blood, which enables us to overcome sin, sickness and disease by the blood of the Lamb and by the word of our testimony. (Revelation 12: 11). Today by faith receive your healing from Yehovah Rapha, the LORD who heals!

Day 9 – Remember

But you shall remember the LORD your God, for it is He who gives you power to get wealth, so that He may confirm His covenant which He has sworn to your fathers, as it is today.
Deuteronomy 8:18

We must always remember that every good and perfect gift comes from God. (James 1:17) Many times when people are in a bad place or need divine assistance, they cry out to God, and God delivers them or makes a way of escape. They may say, "LORD if you make a way out of no way, I will serve you, or I will give back to you." The interesting thing that occurs is after God makes a way of escape is that people can get amnesia and forget God. The LORD told the children of Israel that they should remember that it was the Lord who brought them through the wilderness. (Duet 8:2) And because it was the Lord who supplied all of their needs, they should keep the commandments of the Lord. Why? Because it is the Lord who gives us health, wealth, peace, and strength. It is the Lord who gives us all things freely to enjoy. (1 Tim 6: 17) Let us always remember that it is the Lord who gives us the power to get wealth or to accomplish anything noteworthy. We came into this world with nothing and we shall leave without it. (1 Tim 6: 7) Today remember the LORD by giving him thanks and praise for all that he has done in your life!

Day 10 – Release

> At the end of every seven years you shall make a release, and this is the manner of the release. Every man who has a loan to his neighbor shall release it. He shall not exact it from his neighbor, or from his brother, because it is called the LORD's release.
> Deuteronomy 15:1-2

Wouldn't it be wonderful if this law applied today? I mean there would be no need to file bankruptcy! Every creditor that you owe, every debt that is hanging over your head would be released in Jesus name to bring freedom from debt and the lender! Well, since we have been redeemed from the curse of the law of sin and death, we are no longer under the law in which this principle was given. Yet, when we think about this principle, it was a merciful principle indeed under the Old Covenant! God provided a way of escape from the lender and life destroying debt! The law came through Moses, but grace and truth came through Jesus Christ. (John 1: 17) When Christ died at the cross, he said, "It is finished!" Which meant the debt and weight of sin through the sacrificial death and blood of Jesus Christ is complete, accomplished, performed and paid in full! Jesus paid the price for us. You are free in Jesus name! Today let us also pray for release from physical debt to be financially free in Jesus name, that you may owe no man anything but love! (Rom 13: 8)

Day 11 – Resurrection

Jesus said to her, "I am the resurrection and the life. He who believes in me, though he may die, he shall live. And whoever lives and believes in me shall never die. Do you believe this?"
John 11:25-26

The resurrection of our LORD Jesus Christ is an important doctrine of our faith. Because if Christ is not raised, our faith is vain and we are still in sin according to the Apostle Paul! (1 Cor 15-17) Jesus said, "I am the resurrection and the life" which means that he is the giver of life. Jesus also said, "I lay down my life, that I might take it again. I have the power to lay it down and the power to take it again." (John 10-17-18) In other words, I have the power to give death and give life! Child of God, is there anything in your life that needs resurrection? Today believe God to resurrect it and give life to it again! The Prophet Ezekiel was in the valley of dry bones which was full of death. The Lord then commanded him to prophesy the Word to the dry bones that they would live. (Eze 37:3-7) He then commanded Ezekiel to prophesy to the four winds that they would breathe and live again! (Eze 37:9) So I prophesied as he commanded me, and breath came into them, and they lived, and stood up upon their feet, an exceeding great army.(Eze 37:10) Today, by faith, declare the Word over every life situation you may have, and command it to live again!

Day 12 – Revive

For thus says the High and Lofty One Who inhabits eternity, whose name is Holy: "I dwell in the high and holy place, with him who has a contrite and humble spirit, to revive the spirit of the humble, and to revive the heart of the contrite ones.
Isaiah 57:15

Isn't it amazing that God who is high and lifted up and inhabits eternity would leave his heavenly abode and dwell with mankind? The Bible says that Jesus, the living Word became flesh and dwelled among us, and we beheld his glory, the glory as of the only begotten of the Father, full of grace and truth! (John 1:14) The Lord through Isaiah said, "I live high above the heavens and the earth, and inhabit eternity, but I will dwell with them that are of a humble and contrite spirit!" God does not dwell among the proud, haughty and high-minded. He dwells with the humble and the meek. The Bible says in Matt 23:12, "And whoever exalts himself will be humbled, and he who humbles himself will be exalted." The Lord is saying that those that humble themselves he will lift up high, and those that exalt themselves he will bring low. God will always be among those that are of a humble and contrite spirit. Today humble yourself under the mighty hand of God, that he may exalt you in due season!

Day 13- Reconcile

> And having made peace through the blood of his cross, by him to reconcile all things unto himself; by him, I say, whether they are things in earth, or things in heaven.
> Colossians 1:20

Jesus Christ paid the price at the cross of Calvary with his own blood. He not only redeemed us, but reconciled us. The Bible says that the without the shedding of blood there is no remission of sins. (Heb 9:22) Reconcile means to settle a disagreement, or to restore harmony or friendship. Christ reconciled us to himself, when we were in sin and worthy of death. The Bible says that the wages of sin is death. (Rom 6:23) So Christ death, blood, and resurrection paid the price for you and me. This is why at the cross he could say, "It is finished!" In other words, the debt is paid and the wages of sin have been paid in full! As a result the Father committed all things to the Son and we now have peace through our LORD Jesus Christ! Receive by faith your peace today as a result of the blood of Jesus, and his reconciliation at the cross on our behalf.

Day 14- Render

What shall I render to the LORD for all His
benefits toward me?
Psalm 116:12

We often say that God is good all the time, all the time God is good! Jesus told the rich young ruler in Matt 19:17, "Why do you call me good? No one is good but One, that is, God." If we really believe this to be true, and we know that it is, we should give God all the glory, honor and praise that due his name! We should also give back to the LORD everything that we have, including our time, talents and treasure. Truth be told, we are only giving to him what belongs to him. The Bible says that everything that is seen is temporary, and the things that are unseen are eternal. (2 Cor 4:18) David said something so profound in Psalm 116:12! David said, "What can I give back to the Most High God for all his benefits toward me?" "What can I give back to the eternal God of heaven and earth who owns it all?" Two things I believe we can render back to the LORD for his goodness, grace and mercy and they are: 1. Worship him in spirit and in truth, and 2. Be faithful to him in all our ways! Today take the time to worship the LORD in the beauty of his holiness and to be faithful in service and servitude unto the LORD!

Day 15 – Revelation

That the God of our Lord Jesus Christ, the Father of glory, may give to you the spirit of wisdom, and revelation in the knowledge of Him.
Ephesians 1:17

The Apostle Paul in his letter to the Ephesian church prayed an awesome prayer for the people of God, because of their faith and love for Jesus Christ, and all the Saints. This is truly wonderful! Paul heard this about them, and as a result he prayed that the God of our Lord Jesus Christ, the Father of glory, would give them the spirit of wisdom and revelation in the knowledge of Him. There is much more that he prayed, but isn't this what we all need as believers in Christ? The spirit of wisdom and revelation in the knowledge of Jesus Christ! Every believer needs wisdom from on high. Not just earthly wisdom, but spiritual wisdom that comes from the Holy Spirit and revelation! It's not that we need new revelation; we need the revelation that has already been revealed about Christ! Too many times, believers are looking for new revelation, but there is revelation in the Bible concerning Christ from Genesis to Revelation that needs to be unlocked! Why do we need new revelation, when the old revelation still needs to be revealed to us! My prayer is the same as Paul's for you today! "That the God of our Lord Jesus Christ, the Father of glory, may give you the spirit of wisdom and revelation in the knowledge of Him."

Day 16 – Reward

> But you, when you pray, go into your room, and when you have shut your door, pray to your Father who is in the secret place; and your Father who sees in secret will reward you openly.
> Matthew 6:6

The Bible says that in Heb 11:6, "That without faith it is impossible to please God. For he that comes to God must believe that he is God, and that he is a rewarder of those that diligently seek him." I have two questions for you today? How is your faith and how is your prayer life? This scripture is very important for all of us. When we seek the LORD in prayer, Jesus said we should go into our room, shut the door, and seek the LORD in our secret place concerning whatever is in our hearts, and he will reward us openly. How many of us know that God hears all the prayers of his Saints, but this kind of prayer means that we should take the time to really seek the LORD. It's not just a quick prayer, but a time of getting into the presence of God, and seeking him diligently for the things that are on our heart. Today, find a quiet place of prayer, shut the door, eliminate all the distractions, get into the presence of God, and lift up your prayer requests, and petitions before the LORD! When you do this, God said he would answer your prayers and reward you openly!

Day 17 – Reap

But this I say: He who sows sparingly will also reap sparingly, and he who sows bountifully will also reap bountifully.
2 Cor 9:6

The Apostle Paul gives us some very profound wisdom as it relates to giving. Whether you are generous or stingy in your sowing and giving, you will reap it back. Paul is only confirming what numerous other scriptures in the Bible say about giving. Every believer needs to understand and practice the ministry of giving! Giving is one of the greatest ways to show your love. The Bible says, "God so loved the world that he gave his only begotten Son" in John 3:16. Jesus said in Luke 6:38, "Give and it will be given to you, good measure, pressed down, shaken together, and running over will be put into your bosom. For with the same measure that you use, it will be measured back to you." Paul confirms it again in Galatians 6:7, "Do not be deceived, God is not mocked; for whatever a man sows, that he will also reap." Solomon the wise man even gave us some great wisdom on giving as well in Proverbs 11:24-25 "There is one who scatters, yet increases more; and there is one who withholds more than is right, but it leads to poverty. The generous soul will be made rich, and he who waters will also be watered himself." Today, ask God to give you the spirit of generosity so that you can reap bountifully in Jesus Name!

Day 18 – Righteousness

And do not present your members as instruments of unrighteousness to sin, but present yourselves to God as being alive from the dead, and your members as instruments of righteousness to God.
Romans 6:13

As a believer in Christ, we have been born of the Holy Spirit and washed in the blood of the Lamb. Although we are in the world, we are not of the world. When we were in the world we lived like the world, and presented the members of our body as instruments of unrighteousness. Now that we are born again and living for Christ, we are to live holy, righteous lives in Jesus Christ our LORD. We know longer allow sin to reign over us, but we allow the Holy Spirit to lead us and guide us into all truth. So now we dance for Christ, sing for Christ, and everything we do, we bring glory to God! Remember that Christ took our sin and unrighteousness at the cross and made us righteous in him! So now we are the righteousness of God in Christ Jesus! Paul said in 2 Cor 5:21, "For He made Him who knew no sin to be sin for us, that we might become the righteousness of God in Him." Let us always remember that it is not what we have done, or what we can do that makes us righteous. It was what Jesus Christ done at the cross on our behalf that makes us righteous! Today declare out loud that you are the righteousness of God in Christ Jesus!

Day 19 – Riches

And my God shall supply all your need according to
His riches in glory by Christ Jesus.
Phil 4:19

The Apostle Paul commends the church at Phillipi for their gracious support of his ministry. As a result, he tells them that God will supply all of their need according to His riches in glory by Christ Jesus. It is a wonderful thing to be able to bless others, because God will return the blessing to us. Some people have many riches and even when they see a need, they look the other way. We should never chase after the worlds riches, but we should always seek first the Kingdom of God, and his righteousness and all these things will be added unto us. (Matt 6:33) Although we have gold, silver, diamonds and precious stones in the earth, true riches come from heaven. Let us always seek the true riches that come from heaven, because they will never fade away. Today, let us thank the LORD for supplying all of our need, according to his riches in glory!

Day 20 – Recall

This I recall to my mind, therefore I have hope.
Lamentations 3:21

Have you ever just looked back over all the years of your life and began to cry? Sometimes when I think about all that I have been through, and came through, it brings me joy and gives me hope for the future. This is what the Prophet Jeremiah was thinking about. Although it didn't look good for the nation of Judah, he could recall all the great things that God had done historically for the nation of Israel, and he knew there was great hope because of God's covenant promises. Listen to Lam 3:22-23, "It is of the LORD'S mercies that we are not consumed, because his compassions fail not. They are new every morning, great is thy faithfulness." God is truly great, and greatly to be praised. Whenever you are going through a test, trial, tribulation, or trouble in your life, think back and recall to mind how God brought you through! This will give you hope for the future and give you strength to keep pressing on! Today as you recall and remember all that the LORD has done, give him praise and glory for his faithfulness to his Word and all that he is going to do!

Day 21 – Rain

> Has the rain a father? Or who has begotten
> the drops of dew?
> Job 38:28

How many of us like the rain? There is not a lot of people who like the rain! When we think about rain, we think about a day that is filled with no sun and wetness! But think about this; rain is essential for flowers, plants, vegetables, animals, and humans as well. God has given us this wonderful thing called water which comes down from heaven in its purest form. It has no additives, it has no color, it is not man made, and it comes from God. The LORD in his wisdom asked Job the question, "Has the rain a father?" Of course Job probably didn't want to answer the Most High, but James said that every good and perfect gift comes down from the Father of lights, with whom there is no variation or shadow of turning." In the book of 2 Kings, God stopped the rain for three and a half years because of the sin of the people, which produced a serious drought! (1 Kings 17:1 and James 5:17) God in his greatness gives us wonderful rain to refresh the earth. Can you imagine if we didn't get rain for a whole year? We should always give God praise and glory for refreshing us with rain from heaven! Ask God today to refresh you with his presence, and that it would be like rain from heaven!

Day 22 – Run

Then the LORD answered me and said: "Write the vision and make it plain on tablets, that he may run who reads it."
Hab 2:2

Each and every person and family should have a vision for their life and future! This is an Old Testament scripture that is timeless! We should all have a vision for our lives that has the following goals; physical, spiritual, financial and personal! The LORD told the Prophet to write the vision and make it plain, that he may run that reads it. God himself gave the Prophet a prophetic word that has blessed believers over the centuries. When we follow the instructions of the LORD, we cannot fail. Have you written your personal vision? Have you read the church vision in which you are a member? And if you have, are you running with it! Today ask the LORD to give you the grace and strength to run for the God given vision for your life, and for the ministry in which you have been assigned to!

Day 23 – Resist

For I will give you a mouth and wisdom, which all your adversaries will not be able to contradict or resist.
Luke 21:15

King David said in Psalm 27: 1, "The LORD is my light and my salvation; whom shall I fear? The LORD is the strength of my life; of whom shall I be afraid?" How many of us know that when the enemy comes against us we do not have to fear? God promises in his Word that he will be with us. Jesus said, "I will never leave you or forsake you!" (Heb 13:5) Not only that, but the LORD will give us words of wisdom that our adversaries will not be able to contradict, or resist that will silence the enemy. Today ask the LORD to anoint your mouth, and give you prophetic words of wisdom that will confound and confuse the enemy in Jesus Name!

Day 24 – Resist - Part 2

Therefore submit to God. Resist the devil and
he will flee from you.
James 4:7

Have you ever heard someone say, "Resist the devil and he will flee from you!" We often quote that verse, but not in its entirety! I want you to know that you can't resist the devil in your own strength! You must first submit yourself to God, resist the devil, and then he will flee from you. It is a two part process that gives you the victory in Jesus name! You must first submit, and then God gives you the grace and power to resist! There is nothing good in this flesh, when we submit to the LORD; he will give us wisdom, knowledge, understanding and power to overcome any temptations that come our way. One of the reasons many Saints cannot get the victory they desire, is because they have not submitted themselves to the LORD! Today, pray the following prayer: "I submit and surrender all to you blessed Savior! I give you my life, my hopes and my dreams in Jesus Name, amen!

Day 25 – Reprove

Preach the word; be instant in season, out of season;
reprove, rebuke, exhort with all longsuffering
and doctrine.
2 Tim 4:2

The Apostle Paul gave Timothy some very good spiritual advice as it relates to sharing the Gospel of the Kingdom. This advice is also good for each and every one of us as believers in Christ, especially if you are a leader in Christ. You must preach the Word! Not your own word, not your own doctrine, but the teaching which was once delivered unto the saints. We must be ready at all times to share, teach or preach the Word of God. We must also reprove, which means to convince, to gently correct, or admonish. All of us have been reproved at some point in our life, and guess what? There is nothing wrong with correction especially as it relates to the Word of God. Proverbs 15:32 says, "He that refuses instruction despises his own soul: but he that hears reproof gets understanding." Today ask the LORD to give you wisdom in the Word to reprove, and give spiritual correction, instruction, and admonishment in Jesus Name!

Day 26 – Rebuke

Open rebuke is better than secret love.
Proverbs 27:5

In today's society, rebuke is not too popular. People don't take to kindly to rebuke, but the scripture says that open rebuke is better than secret love. In other words, I would rather someone tell me the hard truth to help me, than to say they love me, but won't tell me the truth. Is this a true friend? I don't think so. True friends will tell you the truth and will never do anything to hurt you. Sometimes when people tell us the truth about a matter that we don't agree with, we reject it. I don't need secret love; I need those around me to have a pure love that tells me the truth, no matter how much it hurts! Today ask the LORD to give you boldness to speak and tell others the truth in wisdom and love.

Day 27 – Rebuke - Part 2

He that rebukes a man afterwards shall find more favor than he that flatters with the tongue.
Proverbs 28:23

What an amazing scripture! This is why I love the Word of God. The Bible says that if you rebuke a man for the right reason, you will find favor, rather than if you were to flatter a man. Why is this? It would appear that the one who speaks with kind and smooth words would find favor. Not according to the Bible! Why? Because when we rebuke an individual for the right and truthful reasons, we may save a soul from death or from making the wrong decisions. Now compare this to speaking nice flattering words that are wrong and not based on truth. This is harmful! Because we give a false impression based on words that will not benefit the hearer! We should always tell the truth, even if it hurts! Because in the long run, you may save someone from hurt, harm and danger! Today, understand that truthful, loving and wise rebuke is not meant to harm you, but to help you.

Day 28 – Reaching

> Brethren, I count not myself to have apprehended: but this one thing I do, forgetting those things which are behind, and reaching forth unto those things which are before.
> Phil 3:13

Aren't you glad that God gives us new mercies each and every morning? I mean tomorrow is proof that God gives us grace to move on from yesterday's hurts, pains and disappointments. Paul by the wisdom of the Holy Spirit said, "I may not have completed or taken hold of everything that I desire to do, but there is one thing I will do. I will forget about those things that are behind me, and I will reach forth to those things that are before me." Brother, Sister, whatever you may be going through today is only temporary. Whatever you have been through is behind you. It may be painful and the memories may be lingering in your mind. But by the grace of God, let us follow the example of Paul, and forget about those things that are behind, and let us reach forward to take hold of the future things that are before us! Remember that yesterday is history, but what you do today; can change the outcome of your tomorrow! Today, let us keep reaching forward to take hold of everything God has predestined, purposed, and promised for us in his Word.

Day 29 – Respect

At that day shall a man look to his Maker, and his eyes shall have respect to the Holy One of Israel.
Isaiah 17:7

One of the things I was always taught as a young man was to have respect for adults by saying, "Yes Sir and Yes Ma'am." In today's society it is so much different. We don't often see young people rendering the respect to adults as they used to in the past, but respect is something that all us should have for one another, and more importantly for the LORD. We live in a time where people are running to and fro and looking for answers, but the answer can be found in the LORD. The Psalmist said in Psalm 121:1, "I will lift up my eyes to the hills, from where my help comes from." Heb 12:2 confirms it; "Looking unto Jesus the author and finisher of our faith; who for the joy that was set before him endured the cross, despising the shame, and is set down at the right hand of the throne of God." When we are going through a challenge in life, there are a lot resources and people that we can run to, but the greatest help and assistance comes from the Holy One of Israel, who is the LORD! Today take your eyes off your situation, and keep your eyes and mind stayed on Jesus, who is the author and finisher of our faith!

Day 30 – Rock

And he said, the LORD is my rock, and my fortress, and my deliverer. The God of my rock; in him will I trust. He is my shield, and the horn of my salvation, my high tower, and my refuge, my savior; you save me from violence.
2 Samuel 22:2-3

This is such a powerful passage of scripture. The Bible says that the name of the LORD is strong tower, the righteous run to it and they are safe. (Proverbs 18:10) The Bible also says that Jesus is our rock, fortress, deliverer, shield, horn of our salvation, high tower, refuge and Savior. This is why we have no need to fear! We have the greatest protection ever given to mankind. He is our refuge and protection from all hurt, harm and danger! If God be for us, who can be against us? Our trust should always be in Jesus who is the stone which the builders rejected, and has become the Chief Cornerstone. (Psalm 118:22) Today, give God praise for his divine protection and shielding you from the enemy!

Day 31 – Refuge

In God is my salvation and my glory, the rock of my strength, and my refuge is in God.
Psalm 62:7

Everything we need is in Christ! He gave us life through a saving act of grace at the cross of Calvary. His death, blood, burial and resurrection provided salvation for everyone who receives it by faith! Salvation is defined as preservation from destruction, danger or great calamity. Deliverance from enemies, remission of sins, freedom, prosperity and saving grace. Jesus is our ark, and keeps us safe from the storms of life. He is our dwelling place, shields us from the enemy, and he is our refuge! Refuge is defined as shelter or protection from danger or distress. Today take refuge in the one who is well able to make all grace abound toward you. Take time and give God glory and praise for his great grace, and divine protection from dangers seen and unseen!

Day 32 – Rise

Which is easier, to say, 'Your sins are forgiven you,' or to say, 'Rise up and walk'? But that you may know that the Son of Man has power on earth to forgive sins"—He said to the man who was paralyzed, "I say to you, arise, take up your bed, and go to your house."
Luke 5:23-24

In today's verse, we see the miracle working power of Jesus Christ! The miracle working, resurrection power of our LORD Jesus Christ will cause us to rise up from the depths of despondency, dismay, discouragement and depression. God has spoken the Word, but we must take hold of it by faith. Notice in the scripture that Jesus gave him the Word, but he had to release this faith and take hold of it.
It is the same today. What are you waiting on? Why are you still discouraged? Arise, get up and move forward by faith. This man was paralyzed, and I am sure that all that was within him said, "You have been laying on this bed for many years. How can I get up? Well, if Jesus, the Son of Man said it, we should believe and receive it by faith that it is already done. Today, by faith, get up and get moving into your destiny. Don't lay there another day! Trust God that it is already done, and know without a shadow of a doubt that God has already made you whole; spirit, mind, body and soul!

Day 33 – Reverse

"God is not a man that He should lie, nor a son of man, that He should repent. Has He said, and will He not do? Or has He spoken, and will He not make it good? Behold, I have received a command to bless; He has blessed, and I cannot reverse it."
Numbers 23:20

The Word of the LORD today should encourage each and every one us to stand strong on the promises of God! One thing I have found over the many years is that God is not a man that he should lie. Now I have known many people who have broken their promises or commitments to me, but not God. The Bible says that it is impossible for God to lie. (Heb 6:18) If God said it, you can rest assured that he will bring it to pass. God keeps his covenant promises and everything he said in his Word shall come to pass. As a matter of fact, God has given us his Word and he will not reverse it. How many of us have known people to say one thing and do another? I am so glad that God will do exactly what his Word says he will do. Today, receive by faith the covenant promises of God which are yes and amen for your life! (2 Cor 1:20)

Day 34 – Relieve

If any believing man or woman has widows, let them relieve them, and do not let the church be burdened, that it may relieve those who are really widows.
1 Timothy 5:16

The business of the church is taking care of God's people. Let us never forget that. Sometimes we get so caught up in trying to take care of the community outside the church, we forget about our own in the church. James said, "Pure and undefiled religion before God and the Father is this: to visit orphans and widows in their trouble, and to keep oneself unspotted from the world." (James 1:27) The Bible says that family should relieve the widows if possible, so that the church can assist those who really need the assistance, and help of the church. If there are family members who can assist in this endeavor, it should be done, so that the church can attend to those who are widows of age, disabled, or financially unable to care for themselves. Today, ask the LORD to put someone on your heart. Call or see about them, and give them a word of encouragement with love in Jesus name!

Day 35 – Replenish

And God blessed Noah and his sons, and said unto them, be fruitful, and multiply, and replenish the earth.
Genesis 9:1

One of the things that we know about the LORD is that he is a God of multiplication! One of the first things that he told Adam and Eve was to be fruitful and multiply, and replenish the earth! This is how we know that God has established a thing in the earth. Can it multiply? Does it have the ability to reproduce? Is it fruitful? In the Bible there are stories of women who were barren like Sarah, Hannah, and Rachel, but God graced them to be able to bear children who were mighty men in the earth! Even if you feel as though you are not bearing fruit spiritually, ask the LORD to bless your life, so that you can be fruitful and multiply! Jesus said in John 15:5 "I am the vine, you are the branches. He who abides in me, and I in him, bears much fruit; for without me you can do nothing." As a believer in Christ, always stay connected to the source of life who is the way, the truth and the life! (John 14:6) Today, pray that the LORD give you the ability to be fruitful and to multiply, bearing spiritual fruit in Jesus Name!

Day 36 – Rejoice

Rejoice with those who rejoice, and weep with those who weep.
Romans 12:15

This is a wonderful passage of scripture. We are the body of Christ and we are one in Jesus name. What affects one part of the body, affects the entire body. Have you ever broken a bone, or had chronic pain in your body? The pain affected your entire body. This is why when one member of the body of Christ rejoices, we should rejoice with them. When they weep, we should weep also. Why? Because we are a body of believers who are one in Jesus name. The Bible says in 1 Cor 12:12,"For as the body is one and has many members, but all the members of that one body, being many are one body, so also is Christ." How can we say that are part of the body of Christ and have no regard for one another? Let us never forget that there is one church, but there are many communities of Christ. The Bible says in Eph 4:5-6, There is one Lord, one faith, one baptism, one God and Father of all, who is above all, and through all, and in you all. As we can see, there is only one church and it is the ecclesia, the Body of Christ! Today, pray for someone in the body of Christ that you do not know by faith. Pray that the LORD bless them and cause his face to shine upon them!

Day 37 – Refine

I will bring the one-third through the fire, will refine them as silver is refined, and test them as gold is tested. They will call on my name, and I will answer them. I will say, 'This is my people'; and each one will say, 'The LORD is my God.'
Zechariah 13:9

All of us go through tests, trials, tribulations, temptations and troubles. Just as silver is refined, and gold is tested, God uses situations and the circumstances of life to refine and test us as well. Remember when you were in school? You had to take tests to go to the next grade or level. As it is in the natural, so it is in the spiritual. If you are in the fiery furnace, call on the name of the LORD! He knows what you are going through, and will not let the fire burn you up! The test and trial is not meant to destroy you, but to refine you as silver, gold and precious stones. God wants you to pass the test! Just know that when the testing is complete, God will bring you through and you will come forth as pure gold. Paul said that we should endure hardship like a good soldier of Jesus Christ (2 Tim 2:3). Today, ask the LORD to give you the strength and grace to overcome every test, trial, tribulation, temptation and trouble, so that you can come forth as 24 karat gold!

Day 38 – Regeneration

Not by works of righteousness which we have done, but according to His mercy He saved us, through the washing of regeneration and renewing of
the Holy Spirit.
Titus 3:5

The work of salvation is a spiritual work that came by the death, burial and resurrection of Jesus Christ. Today there is a belief among people that there are many ways to God. The Bible says in Acts 4:12, "Nor is there salvation in any other, for there is no other name under heaven, given among men by which we must be saved." Blood was shed for you and me at the cross of Calvary, and through the power of Holy Spirit we were made new or regenerated in Jesus Christ. John the Baptist, who came before Jesus Christ said in Mar 1:8, "I indeed baptized you with water, but He will baptize you with the Holy Spirit." If you have been born again of the spirit, there was a process of regeneration that took place. In other words you were regenerated, or renewed, which means you are now a new creature in Christ Jesus, born of the spirit, and washed in his blood. Today, celebrate your regeneration and renewal in Christ by the power of the Holy Spirit. Today, let us remember that your citizenship is in heaven and you have been translated into the Kingdom of God. As a result, all of heavens blessings and the benefits of salvation in Christ, belong to you and me!

Day 39 – Rescue

Lord, how long will you look on? Rescue me from their destructions, my precious life from the lions.
Psalm 35:17

In this Psalm, King David in his appeals to the Most High God is crying out to the LORD for deliverance from his enemies. He also compares his adversaries to lions who are ready to devour him. The Apostle Peter in his letter to the church said the devil walks about like a roaring lion, seeking whom he may devour. (1 Peter 5:8) Have you ever cried out to the LORD because of situations in your life that overwhelmed you! I want you to know that God hears the cries of his beloved children. In Luke chapter 18, Jesus tells the story of a woman who cried out to an unjust judge and asked him to give her justice against her adversary! The Bible says he wouldn't do it for a while, but she kept asking for justice and eventually she got it. Then Jesus spoke and said in Luke 18:7-8, "And shall God not avenge His own elect who cry out day and night to Him, though He bears long with them? I tell you that He will avenge them speedily. Nevertheless, when the Son of Man comes, will He really find faith on the earth?" Today, keep the faith, cry out to the LORD and ask him to grant you justice against your adversary! I tell you the truth as a witness; God the Righteous Judge will answer you speedily!

Day 40 – Recompense

A man will be satisfied with good by the fruit of his mouth, and the recompense of a man's hands will be rendered to him.
Proverbs 12:14

One of the most interesting and profound topics in the Bible is about the mouth and the tongue. Do we really understand that death and life are in the power of the tongue? Jesus said in Matt 12:36-37, "But I say to you that for every idle word men may speak, they will give account of it in the Day of Judgment. For by your words you will be justified, and by your words you will be condemned." Now if Jesus said this, don't you think we need to heed this advice? The scripture says that a man or woman will be satisfied with good, by the fruit of their mouth. In other words, you will have what you say. This is not about name it, or claim it! This is what the Bible says about the fruit that comes from your mouth, and whether it is good or bad, you will have what you say. The scripture also says that the recompense of a man's hand will be rendered to him. Recompense means to repay, or compensate. It means to make return of something for anything given or done. This scripture is really speaking of sowing and reaping. Whatever you sow with your mouth and hands you will recompense or receive back. Today consider this scripture, and make adjustments in your life to reap a harvest in Jesus name!

Praise God! This is the completion of 40 days of restoration! I pray that the LORD bless you richly!

Here is how you can receive Jesus Christ as Lord and Savior:

1. Admit your need (I am a sinner).
2. Be willing to turn from your sins (Repent of your sins).
3. Pray and believe in your heart and confess with your mouth that Jesus Christ is Lord. (Believe and receive Jesus Christ as Lord and Savior)
4. Be baptized in the Name of Jesus for the remission of your sins and you shall receive the gift of the Holy Spirit. (Be filled with the Holy Spirit)

How to Pray:
Heavenly Father, I come to you in the Name of Jesus. I confess and repent of my sins. I believe in my heart and confess with my mouth that Jesus is Lord. I believe that you died on the cross for my sins. You were buried and resurrected on the third day. Come into my heart and life. Fill me with your precious Holy Spirit. Today I believe and receive Jesus Christ as my Lord and Savior. In Jesus Name! Amen.

This is just the beginning of a wonderful new life in Jesus Christ. To deepen this relationship you should: Read your Bible every day to know Christ better. Communicate with God in prayer every day. Tell others about Christ. Worship, fellowship, and serve with other born again Spirit filled Christians in a church where Christ and the true Gospel are preached. As Christ's representative in the world, demonstrate your new life by your love and concern for others. The Bible says, "Let your light so shine, that others may see your good works and glorify your Father in heaven. Matt 5: 16.

About the Author

Pastor Jamal E. Quinn is the Senior Pastor of Firm Foundation Christian Fellowship in Riverview, FL. He is a native of Louisville, Kentucky and a U.S. Navy veteran of 21 years.

He accepted the call into the ministry and was licensed as a Minister of the Gospel of Jesus Christ in 1999. In May 2002 - 2003, while serving in the military he was ordered to the Middle East with Special Operations Command Central Forward on a one-year assignment in Doha, Qatar. It was at this time while serving in the desert, that the Lord called him to preach the Gospel and minister the Word of God in True Righteousness, Holiness, Deliverance and Truth.

In June 2003, he was assigned to Naval Air Station Jacksonville, Florida on another assignment. During this time he committed himself to a thorough and diligent study of the Holy Bible. In September of 2005, he retired after serving 21 years in the U.S. Navy.

In Oct 2005, he returned home to Riverview, Florida where the Lord led him to start a community Bible study by faith. Preaching and teaching the Gospel in his neighborhood to anyone that had an ear to hear. In Oct 2007, after faithfully conducting a Bible study group in his home, the Lord called Pastor Jamal and Prophetess Sheryl Quinn to plant Firm

Foundation Christian Fellowship in the community of Riverview.

Pastor Quinn is a visionary, shepherd, and watchman who preaches the Gospel of the Kingdom with passion, power and truth. Pastor Quinn's passion is teaching, exhorting and encouraging the Body of Christ to fulfill their God ordained destiny, and to live their lives as examples in Jesus Christ.

He received his Associate of Science Degree at Excelsior College, Albany, New York, and obtained his Bachelor of Arts in Pastoral Ministry from South Florida Bible College and Theological Seminary in Deerfield Beach, FL.

Pastor Quinn has been married to Co-Pastor and 1st Lady Sheryl Quinn, his high school sweetheart for 34 years. For additional information on Pastor Quinn or other books, visit https://jamalquinn.com/
For additional information on Firm Foundation Christian Fellowship, visit https://www.firmfoundationcf.org

www.ingramcontent.com/pod-product-compliance
Lightning Source LLC
Chambersburg PA
CBHW061301040426
42444CB00010B/2466